BRUISER'S
G'day at the Park

Diana Smith
ILLUSTRATED BY JULIE LEIMAN WEAVER

First Published 2020 by
Books to Inspire
Perth, Western Australia

Text © by Diana Smith
Illustrations © by Julie Leiman Weaver
Edited by Brooke Anne Olive

The right of Diana Smith and Julie Leiman Weaver to be
identified as the author and illustrator respectively
of this work has been asserted by them in
accordance with the Copyright Act 1968.

All rights reserved
ISBN: 978-0-6489970-1-6 hc
978-0-6489970-2-3 sc

www.dianasmithbookstoinspire.com

BRUISER'S
G'day at the Park

Written by Diana Smith
Illustrated by Julie Leiman Weaver

Bruiser wakes up early every day.
He grabs his ball and wants to play.

He yawns and gives a big stretch.
Let's go outside, it's time to play fetch!

On with his collar, on with his lead,
And out the door with the greatest speed.

Bruiser wanted to race and he
wanted to win.
"Come for a run?" he asked with a grin.

But have you ever seen a kangaroo hop?
They bounce up and down
and never stop.
A mob of roos move so incredibly fast.
So of course, poor Bruiser came last.

Under the trees, Bruiser sniffed
without a care.
Up above galahs squawked as they
rose in the air.

"How high can you fly?" they
screeched at him.
But Bruiser was sad, he had no wings!
Cackling and chattering,
they flew up and away.
Leaving Bruiser below, on the ground
he must stay.

Over the hill, and then along the stream,
The little puppy explored
through shadows and sunbeams.
Suddenly Bruiser discovered
a curious scent!
Running quickly now,
through the bushes he went.

In a little clearing he found a shimmering, shining pond, With flowers and ferns and green luscious fronds.

"Want to play?" croaked a
sweet little frog.
Leaping from a shiny lily pad
onto a small brown log.

"Yes please," said Bruiser,
jumping right in.
But oh no, we forgot,
Bruiser can't really swim!
Bruiser was wet and Bruiser was sad.
Falling in the pond made him feel bad!

Bruiser was tired and curled up for a nap.
From far above he heard a
pop, crunch and snap!
Looking way up high, through
the branches of the trees,
He saw a colony of koalas
munching on gum leaves.

Now Bruiser was lonely,
and he wanted to chat,
But dogs cannot climb that high,
it's a known fact!

Chasing his ball, Bruiser sped
back over the grass.
It seemed his time at the park
had gone by so very fast.
Yet the day was still warm,
the day was still bright.
This little puppy just wanted
to soak up the sunlight.
The park was almost empty,
everyone had gone home.
When all of a sudden, his own doggie
friends came to roam!

First was Snoop,
running fast with his stick,
Then Ollie, Max and Ellie
bounded up just as quick.
Now racing and running and
having great fun,
The five little dogs made the
most of the sun!

Bruiser was happy
spending time with his mates.
Any day at the park
spent playing was great!